BROADWAY SONGS FOR TWO

Arrangements by Peter Deneff

ISBN 978-1-5400-1285-2

Hal•Leonard®

7777 W. Bluemound Rd. P.O. Box 13819 Milwaukee, WI 53213

Visit Hal Leonard Online at
www.halleonard.com

CONTENTS

4 **Any Dream Will Do** from *Joseph and the Amazing Technicolor® Dreamcoat*

6 **Bring Him Home** from *Les Misérables*

8 **Cabaret** from *Cabaret*

10 **Edelweiss** from *The Sound of Music*

12 **For Forever** from *Dear Evan Hansen*

14 **Hello, Dolly!** from *Hello, Dolly!*

16 **I Believe** from *The Book of Mormon*

18 **I Whistle a Happy Tune** from *The King and I*

20 **If I Were a Bell** from *Guys and Dolls*

22 **The Impossible Dream (The Quest)** from *Man of La Mancha*

24 **Mamma Mia** from *Mamma Mia!*

26 **Memory** from *Cats*

28 **My Favorite Things** from *The Sound of Music*

30 **One** from *A Chorus Line*

32 **Popular** from *Wicked*

34 **Seasons of Love** from *Rent*

36 **Seventy Six Trombones** from *The Music Man*

38 **Summertime** from *Porgy and Bess®*

40 **Sunrise, Sunset** from *Fiddler on the Roof*

42 **Tomorrow** from *Annie*

44 **Where Is Love?** from *Oliver*

46 **You've Got a Friend** from *Beautiful: The Carole King Musical*

ANY DREAM WILL DO

from JOSEPH AND THE AMAZING TECHNICOLOR® DREAMCOAT

ALTO SAXES

Music by ANDREW LLOYD WEBBER
Lyrics by TIM RICE

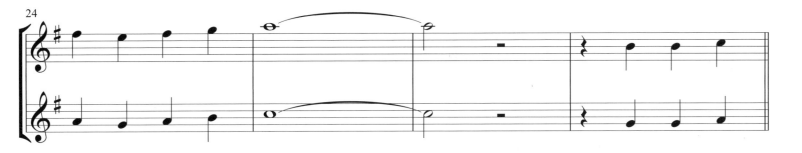

BRING HIM HOME

from LES MISÉRABLES

ALTO SAXES

Music by CLAUDE-MICHEL SCHÖNBERG
Lyrics by HERBERT KRETZMER
and ALAIN BOUBLIL

Slowly, with feeling

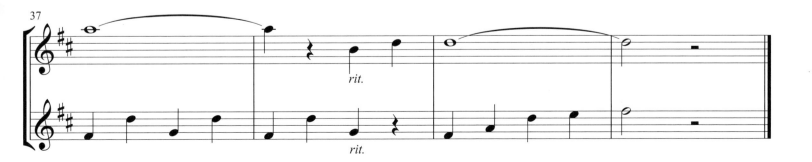

CABARET
from the Musical CABARET

ALTO SAXES

Words by FRED EBB
Music by JOHN KANDER

Moderately

EDELWEISS
from THE SOUND OF MUSIC

ALTO SAXES

Lyrics by OSCAR HAMMERSTEIN II
Music by RICHARD RODGERS

FOR FOREVER
from DEAR EVAN HANSEN

ALTO SAXES

Music and Lyrics by BENJ PASEK
and JUSTIN PAUL

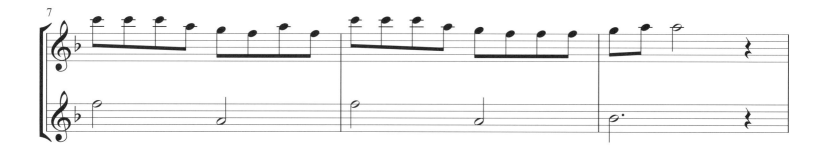

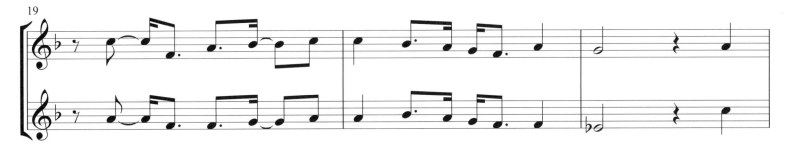

HELLO, DOLLY!

from HELLO, DOLLY!

ALTO SAXES

Music and Lyric by
JERRY HERMAN

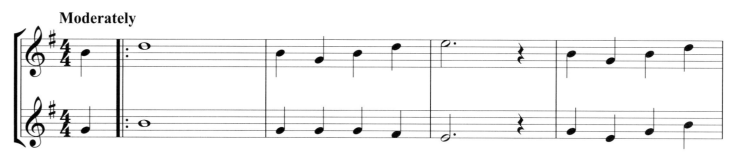

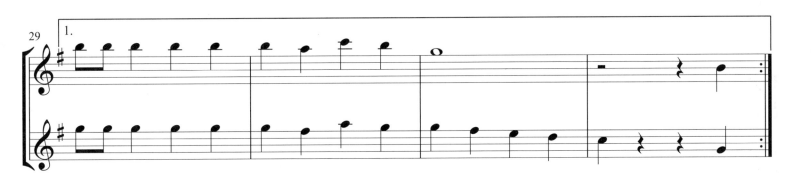

I BELIEVE
from the Broadway Musical THE BOOK OF MORMON

ALTO SAXES

Words and Music by TREY PARKER,
ROBERT LOPEZ and MATT STONE

Moderately

I WHISTLE A HAPPY TUNE

from THE KING AND I

ALTO SAXES

Lyrics by OSCAR HAMMERSTEIN II
Music by RICHARD RODGERS

IF I WERE A BELL

from GUYS AND DOLLS

ALTO SAXES

By FRANK LOESSER

THE IMPOSSIBLE DREAM
(The Quest)
from MAN OF LA MANCHA

ALTO SAXES

Lyric by JOE DARION
Music by MITCH LEIGH

MAMMA MIA
from MAMMA MIA!

ALTO SAXES

Words and Music by BENNY ANDERSSON,
BJÖRN ULVAEUS and STIG ANDERSON

Moderately

MEMORY
from CATS

ALTO SAXES

Music by ANDREW LLOYD WEBBER
Text by TREVOR NUNN after T.S. ELIOT

Slowly, with feeling

MY FAVORITE THINGS
from THE SOUND OF MUSIC

ALTO SAXES

Lyrics by OSCAR HAMMERSTEIN II
Music by RICHARD RODGERS

ONE

from *A CHORUS LINE*

ALTO SAXES

Music by MARVIN HAMLISCH
Lyric by EDWARD KLEBAN

POPULAR
from the Broadway Musical WICKED

ALTO SAXES

Music and Lyrics by
STEPHEN SCHWARTZ

SEASONS OF LOVE

from RENT

ALTO SAXES

Words and Music by
JONATHAN LARSON

SEVENTY SIX TROMBONES

from Meredith Willson's THE MUSIC MAN

ALTO SAXES

By MEREDITH WILLSON

SUMMERTIME
from PORGY AND BESS®

ALTO SAXES

Music and Lyrics by GEORGE GERSHWIN,
DuBOSE and DOROTHY HEYWARD
and IRA GERSHWIN

SUNRISE, SUNSET

from the Musical FIDDLER ON THE ROOF

ALTO SAXES

Words by SHELDON HARNICK
Music by JERRY BOCK

TOMORROW
from the Musical Production ANNIE

ALTO SAXES

Lyric by MARTIN CHARNIN
Music by CHARLES STROUSE

WHERE IS LOVE?

from the Broadway Musical OLIVER!

ALTO SAXES

Words and Music by
LIONEL BART

Slowly, tenderly

YOU'VE GOT A FRIEND

featured in BEAUTIFUL: THE CAROLE KING MUSICAL

ALTO SAXES

Words and Music by
CAROLE KING